First published i
GW00385096

© **2022 b**

To find out more about the author and his works, visit his

YouTube channel Luain Press, or find him on Instagram:

luainpress. You can also find his other work on

Amazon.com.

Two Old Ghosts on Pembroke Road contains a reference to

If Ever You Go to Dublin Town by Patrick Kavanagh.

Edited by Alison Cummins.

Cover designed by More Visual Ltd.

ABOUT THE AUTHOR

Lee Sheridan (1996-) is an Irish novelist, short story writer, and poet. In 2022, he established Luain Press – a small online publishing house that aims to promote the works of aspiring writers. When he is not writing, he is a teacher of English and Religious Education. His debut novella, *St George's Day*, was published in 2022.

MONUMENTS

& OTHER POEMS

By

Lee Sheridan

To Serge,

from G

3

This collection is dedicated to Mam and to Dad.

CONTENTS

Part I – Degeneracy

CONTENTS

Part II – Purity

Part I – Degeneracy

Tamed Country

I pity the fenced horses

And long for that faraway land:

That place where there's no roads

To lead you home; no names, no signs

Or townlands to roam.

No area of land bound by sounds of the

Tongue, only trees upon trees –

All the squirrel needs: a bridge above soil

Between east and west, the crest and its nest.

I hear the cries:

O, tame me not, name me not;

Let me wander unfenced and free;

No signs to guide, only my heart to lead.

In O'Neill's

Memories made over years gone by;

Beneath this roof where youth was shy,

To where I stand now, I look around;

At every corner, a memory found:

An earnest glance, there and there;

A pint with a grandparent, no longer here;

The touch of hands across tables, and

Hushed talk on those rare quiet nights.

Each corner of this place a cornerstone:

An imprint upon my life.

Nono

Nono, you must know

That you are the best;

God's love spills out

From the heart in

Your chest.

Your house was a heaven

In my early childhood years.

I think over those sweet times

And am reduced to tears.

Playing in the garden

On a hot summer's day,

Building cardboard castles

And finding dragons to slay.

Climbing up the walls

And rolling in the grass;

Coming in for tea

And going with you to mass.

Forsaken you must feel

In the recent years gone by.

For this, I am truly sorry,

For this, I cry.

But Nono, you must know

That you are with me all the time;

Bound together in stillness,

Your spirit one with mine.

Things I Deem Essential

A wooden desk, at least

two drawers on the left,

and a space underneath for books and other things.

Yellow sticky notes; a small black journal;

a cup to hold various pens; a bottle opener;

Sellotape; a small stone – lapis lazuli –

next to a candle of lemongrass and cedarwood –

scented like Bloom's soap, still wrapped and

waiting by the desk lamp.

Low lighting; a heater by the feet; a swivel chair;

Kavanagh's selected poems; *At-Swim-Two-Birds*;

a cookbook for students; and *Ulysses* –

all stacked next to a box of paracetamol, that sits

beside a mass card, that contains a photo of a loved one

Lost.

Two Old Ghosts on Pembroke Road

It was a mark of intimacy to be admitted there,
For whatever the reason, said Cronin.
After my visit in 2019, I now see those words
As an omen.

I remember well that cold Christmas night:
The snowless street, faintly lit, and upon the
First floor sill, no wing mirror in sight.

Inside, bright; the fire alive and warm;
Baileys and porter for everyone, and the
Kitchen abuzz like a swarm.

The table had been laid, and the sumptuous food
Brought out; we were stuffed to our windpipes,
Till our belts were giving out.

Two candlesticks stood proudly on the table;
We held our drinks level to their flames, and
Made a toast to Grandad's ghost, when one
Popped out of its holder.

13

Went with earthly hands to fix it, but out it came again;

Dismissed it in the moment, before remembering

Kavanagh's request to look out for his ghost,

Dishevelled with shoes untied. I thought of him and

Grandad smiling down on me from heaven,

And my spirit was filled with pride.

Schönbrunn

Went for a stroll about Schönbrunn
– a poet's Eden, may I say;
with its secret gardens and Greek statues,
to soak it in took us the day.

Hot high sun and scented flowers; reds and
pinks with yellows and whites;
three or four gargantuan fountains: a bright
abundance of beautiful sights.

And amid the pretty winding paths, hidden
treats are to be found: small cafés with cakes
and lemonades, amidst bushes from which
red squirrels bound.

I felt a richness from that day, that I knew
I would never feel from that place thereon:
how predictable it is, that this new innocence,
this paradise, is taken from me, is gone.

May Love

Her mouth was pressed to me,

As we lay there in bed;

Lips, so gentle, against my

Sleeping head.

And outside, around, all was

Slow and still –

But inside, alive, all was

Such a thrill.

Monuments

I look out the 67, and every second day,

I see that a pigeon is perched on O'Connell's

White head – his head whiter than any of the

Angels that sit below him.

And along the Liffey, I see Anna Livia in her

Secluded spot. "The Floozie in the Jacuzzi" they call her.

Pennies are tossed at her, as are condoms.

Such things are washed away overtime,

Just like the wishes, water off her back.

She had a nice view of O'Connell before being

Moved. With nothing to look at but the

Back of his white head, I imagine that she would

Have thought of him as a kindred spirit, and that she

Would have felt comforted by him.

But her heart is made of bronze, and her pains grow only in
me.

Featherless Phoenix

Dust before

And dust after;

Rise from the ash

And fall.

Or so they say.

Now featherless,

I can no longer fly;

I can barely nip

At the low-hanging fruits –

And when I do,

They taste bitter

And dry.

Once plump and

Waxy,

And filled firm with juice,

18

They tasted like life

In my mouth.

Now they taste of ash –

The little liars!

Their texture: grey

Flakes and dust.

Choking, coughing

Hawking!

Gasping greedily

At the grey cindery air.

Fill me, lift me –

Help me soar!

But the wings,

Now featherless,

Are no more.

Exiles

A man stood on Dún Laoghaire pier

when a vision came to mind:

'Should I stay or go from here?

Can I leave this place behind?'

And a fellow jackeen, years before,

with a Galway girl by his side,

said, 'We can't stay here anymore,

a new land we must find.'

So farewell dear Dublin,

and goodbye Galway Bay.

We'll find ourselves a new land

a long, long way away.

These two men met in Paris

and soon they formed a bond.

Of this new place they lived in,

they both grew very fond.

Though away from home in body,

it never left their minds;

pushing pens was their hobby,

and towards home, they were kind.

But while it was their calling

to leave this unfair place,

and though I know it's fallen,

in my eyes, it's saved by grace.

And leave it I could not,

for it's the land that mothered me,

and I, being its son, could not

leave it free.

So, hello dear Dublin,

and how are you, Galway Bay?

In this land we'll find ourselves,

at the dawning of the day.

Photo of a Dead Man I Revere

A four-cornered wishing well. Is that all I am?

I smile out at you, but you seem to be searching

For something more.

You are haunted by what were my perceptions;

They have not been buried with me.

I maintain a hold on you; my opinion still holds weight.

You look at me and smile when you are on track or do

Right. Other times, you turn away; you take a seat and be

Quiet.

You base your moods on me, a mere image in a frame.

What you do makes no difference;

To me, it's all the same.

Flower

See now,

The flower of her breast

Rising

Towards the shadows

Of her collarbone and

Her sunkissed shoulders –

Jealous that the sun can

Place its hot lips upon them

Without condition. Sweat-salted

Cheek dimples, round warm and brazen,

Like the fragrance that follows her:

Amber patchouli, pink pepper,

Jasmine and vanilla.

See now, see far, the soft touch

Of tendril fingers; ticklish and electric.

Goosebumped skin, sparks deep within –

Waving through the windows of her hazel eyes.

God's Face

A world within water is wavy and true,

What shows on its surface is wont to imbue:

A silence, a stillness; a change in the mind

The rock that is spirit is what one will find.

Morning Meditation – *for John Butler*

In Bakewell,

When the sky is blue-black,

When all is quiet,

Cross over the road

To the Church.

Move with purpose,

With a blanket underarm

As the Church is cold.

Be quick to sit with feet on the floor,

With your bottom on the chair.

Be still and know God, and

Move out without form;

Meltaway from this place,

This world, forlorn.

Brush over all you know

With this ethereal paint;

Realise that the worst sinners

Were the greatest saints.

Part II – Purity

The Place to Be

If you're looking for a place that's cheap,

With litter as far as the eye can see;

If you don't mind missing out on sleep,

Then Athlone town is the place to be.

If you don't mind waking up to the cold,

With your shivering face as white as a sheet;

If you don't mind coughing due to mould,

Then Athlone town is the place to be.

If you don't mind housemates stealing your food,

With the sight of dirty dishes, a guarantee;

If you don't mind your good nature being abused,

Then Athlone town is the place to be.

If you're used to the sky being grey and bleak,

And the chance of contracting an STD;

If you're used to four or five takeaways a week,

Then Athlone town is the place to be.

But if you're forsaken and your wits are at their end,

I think you'll have to agree:

There's always someone you can call a friend,

In the town of Athlone, the place to be.

Toilet in a Student's House

My bum hovers above the seat,
As I'm too afraid to let the two meet.

No bog roll to wipe my hole,
And no thin plies to shield my thighs.

The seat was once a perfect white –
As pretty as a picture;
Now it's dirty yellow, with curled
Pubes caught in the fixtures.

Each weak flush, a gurgled cry;
No soap to wash your hands, no word of a lie.

The floor beneath your feet is sticky
From congealed beer and piss…

Oh, my clean home-house toilet,
Yes, you I truly miss!

Borrowed Happiness

Dry skin around the knuckles;

Cracked, and bleeding.

Nails that are bitten down too low, and

A wild week that took too much.

On the slow descent now:

High down to a low, in spirit

And in funds. A morose mind is

All I have for company.

The bus drops me off in a town

I can no longer remember; I stroll blindly,

My glassy eyes spying a hopping crow.

Rich memories made in the recent days

Gone by; priceless in the long run –

But what price have I paid now?

The head is heavy at the minute, the soul

Balanced out from false sorrow:

Yes, I had fun the other day, but only because

Of the happiness borrowed from tomorrow.

A Lesson in Patience

'No need to let it settle,' I say.

'Just pour it straight to the top.' (There's

a game of pool in the background, you see,

that, and the bar is busy and hot.

I knew as well that the custom was a direct

result of the Angelus: at six o'clock you'd stop,

no matter what you were at.) She glared at me when

I asked this of her, though; no, she didn't like that.

'I'll get in trouble,' she says, 'I was told off the last

time I did it.' – 'But if the customer doesn't mind,' says I,

'then it hardly makes a difference?'

'It's just not how things are done here,' she says, with a

cold tone of finality. I nod my head and think over this

tradition born from sacred totality.

I could see where she was coming from, and respected it

all the same; I was then made wait for the pint to settle,

and bask in my impatient shame.

Rag Week

In the town of Athlone, I'm never alone;

I've my dreams to stay with me all day.

And when the church bell starts ringing,

Oh, the town will be singing,

For its Rag Week, oh didn't I say?

And down by the Shannon,

Where Sean's bar is hoppin',

I set my eyes upon her,

And my sense, it went missing

When our lips got to kissing,

For its Rag Week, oh didn't I say?

Rag Week, oh, Rag Week,

Tell me the place, I'll be there.

Rag Week, oh, Rag Week,

These rare days, so sweet and so fair.

And on the last night,

When I left her sweet side,

Instinct said I'd surely pay,

And when I came back –

Yes, just like that –

My girl, she was taken away.

So now I'm alone in the town of Athlone,

No friends have chosen to stay,

With my distant old dreams

Lost to the streams, this Rag Week

I've not nothing to say.

But I know in my mind, there will come a time

That all this will come to an end.

With the days quickly passing,

I find myself asking:

When will Rag Week come 'round again?

Rag week, oh, Rag Week,

Tell me the place, I'll be there.

Rag Week, oh, Rag Week,

These rare days, so sweet and so fair.

On The Ferry Back to Inis Óirr

Seasickness at the memory of cold hands
On painted steel bars; the bobbing motion,
Up and down. I think of that dying evening now
And remember when I was a faithful man, a proud
Man – sure of himself.

Trust from her but not from me; a short but
Passionate period of time, so alive with love and
Confused with lust, and her black hair blowing
In the windy night, and her hand
Not far from mine.

And when I did it, I didn't think of her once;
I'm the hypocrite who destroyed her trust.
And she asks me how I could do that, with tears in her
Eyes, like those from her laughter at the hail shower
Coming back from the Plassey.

Inis Óirr, commit me here – forgive me for what
I've done. Let your foamy waters wash over me,
And take these pleasant memories away.

Self Portrait

I

Purple.

Mam's pin-needled arm stretched out over my cot, our pinkies linked, and if broken, by God, the cry.

Long days then. Scattered smiles and blurred sun. Climbing up the mountain of carpeted steps to the landing where all the doors and possibilities were.

I remember being bounced on Mam's knee. I wet myself because she was tickling me. Another time I shoved a finger up her nose without warning. It bled and she frowned but was not angry.

When I was a bit taller, I told a neighbouring child to bury a euro in their garden and it would grow into a money tree. This boy beamed up at me with wide eyes and said he would, and he did, so I dug it up. It was mine now, but it was quickly spent in the one shop.

I kicked a ball once with Dad, on the green. The sun was sinking behind the black treeline of the estate. We were laughing. Dad was a jack of all trades. He could do anything, so long as it wasn't to a perfect standard, and he knew everything. 'Lee,' he'd say. 'Would you give me a hand with this?' I'd help him with all sorts of mad shit. One day Mam came home to us ripping out the fireplace. 'What the fuck are you doing?' she said, distraught. 'I don't like it,' he said. 'I want to put a new one in.' The new one couldn't support a fire. It was purely aesthetical. He hadn't meant for it to be that way, but that's the way it turned out, and for years we went without a functioning fireplace. One day, he got a bedside table and sawed the thing in half. In fairness to him, it was sawed perfectly down the middle, but then he put each half on either side of his bed. If you so much as turned over in your sleep, the thing would fall, and all its contents would spill out across the floor. He was generally calm and cool; Mam, on the other hand, had acid coming up her neck.

I remember shovelling dog poo, and petting my dog, Benjy, and me wanting to pet him but not wanting his smell on my hands. Bathing him didn't seem to rid him of the smell. We came home one October evening and let Benjy in from the back garden. After a while, we noticed a strong smell of rotten egg in the house. We scoured the place against the backdrop of exploding fireworks, sniffing until we found Benjy on his side in the back room, his belly scorched.

In school they played tag. I remember joining in, but after a few moments they were annoyed at me and said they hadn't asked me to play, and I was to leave them alone. I felt I must've done something wrong, so I left them be.

I liked drawing detailed pictures of graveyards. I'd ask Mam to wrap a scarf around my head like your man from *Harry Potter*; then I'd unravel it slowly and pretend Voldemort was on the back of my head, before asking her to wrap it around again. Mam was paying this woman to mind me around this time. Before her, I must've burned out two other childminders. One because I unbuckled my seatbelt and ran out of her car, and the other because I was being collected from school and upon seeing a small bird on the path, remarked, 'I wonder what would happen if I crushed that bird's head?' – 'Your son says strange things,' said the lady. 'I don't want to mind him anymore.'

Dad locked me in a room once because I was bold. I screamed at the door and bashed at it with boxes of toys. I stuck my head out the window in the hopes I'd see a squad car rolling past. It never came, but it didn't have to: Mam let me out after a while.

I loved my sister even before she was born, though when she arrived, I didn't like how people held her and talked about her more than me.

One, two, three, four, five, six, seven – all good children go to heaven!

I shit myself for no reason one evening when I was about nine. I was sitting in between my parents while they were watching TV. I might have done it to get out of going to bed, but it couldn't have been worth it. 'Up to bed now,' said Mam. I stood reluctantly, and my pants started sagging from the weight of the shit – and the bang. 'Jesus Christ, that smell,' she said. 'Did you poo yourself? Get up that stairs now! Get up!' I ran bow-legged up those stairs with moist shit rolling left to right in my pants, and she made me scrub them in the sink. I don't think it did them much good, though.

I used to get the bus to school from the top of my estate. I'd sit on a wall and wait for it to arrive. There were other boys waiting as well, older boys. They'd kick a ball while they'd wait. One of them looked at me one day and said, 'Kick it to him.' They did, but I didn't know what to do with it. I said nothing and kicked it back to them. I got talking to them eventually; I grew to like them. They'd call me gay, but for the most part, I didn't care; I knew I wasn't gay so what did it matter? But they kept calling me that, and one day I said, 'If I was gay, I'd want to do this:' – and I kissed one of the guy's shoulders, and your man freaked out and was all like, 'Aw! Get away from me!' – but in a weird sort of way I was happy; it was like getting revenge, and I didn't feel ashamed or embarrassed. Why punch your enemies when you can kiss them?

Mam found out the lads on the bus were calling me gay. She marched over to the house of the boy whose shoulder I kissed. 'Oh right,' says the mother upon being told. 'I'm very sorry to hear about that. Do you mind me asking, though: does he play the GAA?' – 'I'm sorry?' asked Mam. 'The GAA,' repeated the woman. 'Does he play it?' – 'No,' said Mam. 'No, what's that got to do with anything?' – 'Oh, it's just, if he played the GAA, they probably wouldn't be calling him gay, do you know?'

Conor Cusack, Valerie Mulcahy. I wonder were they called gay when they started playing the GAA?

It was also around that time that I wrote my first "novel". Three hundred words long – a masterpiece, I was sure. And I gave it to Mam to read and her face lit up. 'Did you write that all by yourself?' she asked. 'Yeah,' I said. 'Oh, very good!' she said, and I watched her eyes scan over my work. If she hadn't of reacted that way, I'm not sure I would've written much more.

II

We threw water balloons at cows in a field behind one of the estates. We used to talk of the mysterious farmer and his shotgun, and we'd go running around his fields while leaping over wide hard lumps of bullshit. Throwing rocks at the bullshit was addictive because it was a lighter shade and soft on the inside. One day, we brought an overweight friend with us into the field. He claimed he couldn't climb back over the fences, so the three of us spent a half hour rolling baleage over to a wall to clamber back into the estate. It was hard work, but I felt like a man that day.

I liked girls but they made my throat swell up (among other things). Girls were creatures from a foreign galaxy. I went from an all-boy's school to a school with both boys and creatures from an alien planet. I was out sick the first day, so I had to play catch up with classes and books and lockers, and there were all these girls and I was late to one of the Geography classes and the teacher looked me dead straight in the eyes and said if I ever turn up late like that again, I'll regret it, and I was frightened out of my mind even though she was smaller than me, and later that day I was out on the green playing football (even though I hated football) and I noticed this fuzzy blur in the corner of my eye that wouldn't go away no matter where I looked – even when I went in to tell Mam about it, it was getting worse and it grew and when I closed my eyes there were geometrical shapes, all moving and spinning; I told her this and she knew at once what it was: 'A migraine,' she said. 'You're having a migraine.' She got them all the time and she laid me down in a dark room and put a damp folded facecloth over my eyes and I lay there…

Dull thumping, wave after wave, like a beachhead of pain…

I was waving goodbye to my boyish ways then; I realised the truth that few people care for you. Your mother and your father, your siblings, your grandparents. Some people aren't even that lucky. 'You're lucky,' said Nana, 'if you've one good friend in this life. Nearly everyone else is an acquaintance.'

In front of my mam and my sister, and certain people I liked and would've classed as friends, I could be my true self. I could also be anyone: a master of mimicry; someone who could do any accent or impression.

I brought my sister on adventures to faraway lands. We fought all sorts of creatures together. I was the orchestrator, the conductor, the planner, and the actor. I was her entertainer and she, my muse. Everything was possible and to her I was a hero.

But in school I was shy. And there were girls. Better to be quiet, I remember thinking. If you say nothing, you can do no wrong. And in Science I sat between my friend and this girl, and like me, he was an outcast, but he wasn't shy; he was shameless, but he was chatting away to this girl, with me between them, and when I plucked up the courage to join in the conversation, she told me I was boring and that I should be quiet, and I believed that to be true, so I sank into myself. I had done wrong by being quiet, and I had done wrong by joining in.

Being a class clown is easier than you might think; it's no wonder there's so many of them. I was a good one; I did dares on demand and ate food off the floor. Once, I picked up an unused tampon and began swinging it around in the middle of the canteen. At least they're laughing, I remember thinking, at least you're not boring; better to be laughed at than to be boring, right? And laughter is the way to a woman's heart, surely? I could make people go into convulsions with the things I said and did. I had my small group of friends, but I had all these other people that liked me now because I could make them laugh, and none of them thought I was boring – not even the girl from Science.

When I was thirteen, we moved house. The move wasn't far: the new house was in the same estate, but it had an extra bedroom and an ensuite bathroom. The four of us lived in a tiny granny flat on the side of the house for six weeks; we had to live there because Dad was renovating the house. Mam had acid coming up her neck again when he turned one of the bedrooms into a bathroom, devaluing the house. He was tearing down walls, lifting, hammering, drilling, and moving muscles. Testosterone was pumping through him, and one day Mam called me to ask if I could clean the dishes left in the sink whenever I got home from school. I said I would, but it never happened; I opted to sit on my ass instead, and when Mam came home, she huffed, gave out, and started on them. Dad came in a while later and saw her scrubbing them. 'You all right?' he asked. 'I'm grand,' she said. 'I asked Lee to do these when he came in and he didn't do them.' – 'Little shit,' said Dad. He marched into me with long strides and booming steps. 'Come here to me,' he said, lifting me by the collar and throwing me against the wall. I crumpled like a leaf and fell to the floor. 'Get up!' he yelled. 'Get up!' He was like a tower over me. I couldn't speak; I could barely breathe. Mam rushed in. 'What did you do to him, Ger?' – 'Get up,' he said again. 'On your feet!' – 'Leave him, Ger,' said Mam. And he did.

III

I laid my eyes upon a beauty there: a perfect creature,

Pure and fair. Sallow skinned with rounded cheeks, who

Smiled a smile that left me weak. Her piercing glance

Became all I could see; truly, it trumped all else for me.

Upon a pedestal, I placed her needs; everything else,

Distant memories. I painted our future in my mind;

Infatuated figments born from being blind.

Your earnest smile was lost to time; your love for me was

In decline. Look at what my grandparents had:

Sixty years through good and bad,

But fickle love does burn bright:

Night's stars lost to morning's light.

Tit for tat; this, and that. And I know that women are more than just soft skin and tits, and flower metaphors; they have thoughts, too.

Dad rang me one day and asked if there was a letter addressed to him and Mam. I checked and saw that there was. 'Can you put it under the stairs?' he asked. I did what I was told because he was my dad. It wasn't just the one letter I hid. I hid one every few weeks. Letter after letter. I didn't feel good about it, but I was trying to have his back; I figured it was a problem that he was dealing with in the background. When it came to light, his business was on its knees, and the mortgage arrears were nearly at fifty grand. And after twenty-five years, love between my parents, or whatever was left of it, finally went out the window. Sociopathic separation. As bad as it was, all is forgiven.

Love flitters away, each day that goes by –

One parent's truth is another one's lie.

He's a bad man for rarely seeing his children,

But we're the traitors when we do go to see him.

'She's a bitch for ruining my life.'

Yet he's the one who betrayed his wife.

'Your father's the person who's taking the piss!'

'Your mother's the one who brought it to this.'

With no leg to stand on, he records her at her worst;

In the house, there's a rupture, as things start to burst.

I hear it through my earphones, the fight on the stairs;

This house is a home they can no longer share.

In court, I take the stand to speak out against him;

Again, he asserts that he is the victim.

And if marriage is a tree, I won't go on a limb for it's

Fruits, for one parent's lies are another one's truths.

I was about twenty when I wrote that. Neutrality is no good to anyone; you must pick sides. If you stay on the fence, the skin will be ripped from your arm by barbed wire. The only permanency is impermanency, though, and time rots everything, including hate, thank God. But if you hold onto hate, you can't shake hands and make up, and I can tell you that there's nothing worse for the soul. Grudges grow into every tear, every digestive biscuit, and every U2 song; they eventually become more insufferable than the person who caused them.

Oh, love. What has it become for me?

Little insults peppered throughout your day;

Little love-coals intended to be weightless;

Don't let them burden your back.

They're my safety net; I say them with a smirk,

And you scoff before smiling playfully.

IV

Most of the time, I make a real effort to listen and wholesomely internalise what you have to say. I do try, but I'm a cannibal. A lot of the time I only listen to what you say because I might use it later. I listen when I'm waiting for my turn to speak, and my eyes glisten green when I read something that I wish I had written. This is why I hate good books and poems – my awareness of this does not absolve me; I am the first of sinners, and I regret nothing; everything I've experienced has brought me here.

I spent a lot of time listening to other people. That's okay to a point. Criticism can be good, but I realised something when I got feedback from two separate reviewers on the same piece. They both commented on the line, "A smile sprouted across his face." One said, "Nice phrase." – the other said, "Can you use a phrase that doesn't make me think of a plant?"

I wasn't writing for myself anymore; it was a chore. I was forcing myself to fit into this mould, but I wasn't going in. I was suffocating. So, I moved out, lived with undergraduates, flirted with random women, felt free, and wrote what I wanted. I created myself. As Mam always said, "No one's going to come knocking on your door." I now know that you must go knocking on the doors of others, and if you're lucky, someone will invite you in for tea.

I am a writing desk weasel. I love women but am happy that I was born a man. I am lazy in certain ways. I like gangster movies, Guinness and beer, old buildings and the aesthetic, and nimble pens that allow for a nice cursive flow. I'd pay someone to let me write all day. I'd sit there and write and dream. My favourite dream is of me and the love of my life (and maybe a dog) sleeping in front of a fire in a whitewashed cottage on the Hebrides during a rainstorm. If I could paint this scene from my dream, I would, but I cannot paint well. And that's okay, for poetry can sometimes go where paint cannot.

That is all.

BY THE SAME AUTHOR

St George's Day

Lee Sheridan's debut novella tells the story of a part-time supermarket worker and his search for meaning. Set over a single shift in a supermarket, he must balance mundane work with meditation, imagination, and a mouthy manager.

Printed in Great Britain
by Amazon